Homecoming

Homecoming

Julia Cousins

First published 2014 by
Lyre Books
60 Godstow Road
Oxford OX2 8NY
Tel. 01865 556215
www.lyre-books.co.uk

ISBN 978-1-907651-11-3

Cover Picture: *Jinn* by Freya Purdue 2012 ©

For John and Enid

My very grateful thanks to Jay Ramsay for editing and encouragement, Susanna Geddes for proof reading and gentle suggestions and Freya Purdue for allowing me to use one of her beautiful images for the cover.

Poetry has always been part of my life. It probably got into my blood stream when my mother read Shakespeare over my cradle in the midst of the London blitz. Written intermittently over the years, sometimes with long gaps in between, poetry has become a way of trying to capture the essence of some experience, a way of making a bridge between the seen and the unseen. It has become an integral part of my life's journey.

The poems in the book are roughly in chronological order, although some are grouped because they go together.

FJC

I

1962 -1973

Cut grass scents the air;
birdsong threads soft rain;
the garden enfolds me.

Spring

Not caring which path I took
I wandered through the iron gates
into the park.

Among the houses you can tame the spring,
but here there's no escape
from its uncompromising demands.
So young and delicate the leaves
which yet are blinding fire.
'What is it you want of me?' I cry,
'What is it?'
As if the answer lay
in those green flames
dancing away from me
in the breeze.

The cherry trees, thick with blossom,
intensely white,
awaken in me such a longing
that I hardly know myself.
Oh, let me be strong and simple
as this new-born world.

Wind-blown petals drift
against my face
and slowly fall to earth.

Being late

Damn! Why did I oversleep?
Clutching a piece of toast
I rush downstairs,
the front door slams behind me
(that means trouble later)
then, head down, charge for the tube.

The stitch in my side forces me to stop,
panting, dishevelled, full
of impotent rage against things;
the park railing I clutch
leaves a dirty mark on my glove.

But oh, the sun is warm upon my face
and chequered shadows lie across the grass;
even the dingy houses have a cheerful look,
beside me two dusty sparrows
burst into song.

So, I am late.
The world is singing all around me –
it is a beautiful day,
too beautiful to waste.

Winter Scene

The fog has retreated,
though not sufficiently

to give houses and trees
their own identity again.

The frost lies thickly,
holding the garden motionless,
crystallizing details:

thin stiffened fingers of twig,
bent stalks of grass.

A world drained of colour
except for the sudden dark movement
of a blackbird.

Yet above it rides the sun,
a flaming ball of fire
to warm the heart.

Moonlight

I wake suddenly
to find the familiar room made strange,
haunted by ghost light
and dark rearing shapes of furniture.
Full moon,
a perfect circle, untouched
except by a skein of cloud.

I turn away,
but its disturbing
power remains.
Remote, untroubled beauty
troubles me,
touching some chord of longing,
of remembrance
deep within the heart,
and restless
I lie long awake.

Rosemary's for remembrance...

I remember now,
as though I watched another's grief,
the hot sun in the churchyard
and all the ritual of death.

We left a bunch of rosemary on your grave.

There was no need to fear, as I did then,
that I'd forget, or worse,
not remember you as you really were;
the unquestioning affection, the loving pride,
though rarely outwardly expressed between us,
lay too deep for that.

Re-reading your letters to me,
written so carefully to please a child,
seeing your meticulously sharpened pencils,
or that shapeless, friendly pullover,
I can hardly believe
you won't come quietly back into the room,
as if you'd never been away.

Sometimes indeed,
without my willing it,
you are simply there –
a gentle loving presence.
Against that knowing of the heart
nothing has power:
it is secure forever.

A Day of Heat

A day of heat
laps the garden in stillness.

Beneath a clump of pampas grass
lies an inert length of cat,
utterly relaxed.

A purposeful buzz of fly
hovers by the languid paw.

On a sudden, golden
smouldering eyes
of primitive huntress
fasten on prey.

Unwavering that pellucid gaze
of infinite depths,
until the sleepy eyelids
droop once more,
and the tension dissolves.

Sea Balm

The sea half asleep,
basking in the sun
like a gentle beast;
the waves can hardly
lift themselves to
slide over and caress the sands,
then lazily slip back...

The white line of foam unfurls,
and slides away,
smoothing, soothing the sharp-edged
pebbles of the mind;
leaving it calm and sure.

To A Stray Cat

Thin black cat
with snow-spattered coat,
slinking round dustbins
in the evening gloom,
do not howl and howl.

Thin black cat,
it is of no use
to wind yourself
lovingly round my legs –
I cannot take you in:
they do not allow cats
in my bed-sitting room.

Thin black, little black, sad black cat,
you need a home and fire;
find a corner out of the wind,
and shelter from the cold.
No, do not walk with me down the street,
or run on ahead, then turn to wait for me,
your tail quivering in anticipation.

Piteous ball of fur,
do not howl to the bitter night,
for I cannot take you in.

Florence

Dazzled by paintings, drunk with
rich colour and graceful lines,
I came out of the Uffizi
into streets new-washed with rain,
where Spring sunlight was clear,
uncompromising.

How they must have loved this city,
those painters of the Renaissance!
Through the hills that circle it, now as then,
soft-bloomed with silver-grey olives,
dark with cypress trees,
the kings of their nativities
rode in golden splendour,
come to worship Christ
in a Florentine Bethlehem.

They might have passed, intent, unseeing,
this same old peasant quietly ploughing
behind his two white oxen,
his brown face creased and patient with age;
while at any moment, the skies may again
be filled with triumphant angels,
come to tell of a gentle-faced,
withdrawn Madonna and the Child
lovingly cradled in her arms.

Time is a quiet wind that moves
unhurried through the cypress trees,
and leaves no traces of its passing there.

Farewell

Strange it should come to this,
to our tight-locked fingers
and your mouth warm on mine.

An aching tide of longing
flows through and over me
as the darkness does,
here, by the river, become all rivers,
sliding past me into the night.

It empties me of everything
except that intense awareness of you,
which has no need of words or touch.

So we must part,
but let us do it gently.

Think of me kindly
down the years.

Aftermath

I did not know that I could hate you,
as I do sometimes now,
with savage bitterness.
Oh, it does not last –
the caring goes deeper.

Like some bereft and lonely cat
I prowl my empty house,
haunted and mocked by memories,
uneasily aware of self-pity waiting for me.

But if I feel rejected and a fool,
the one who did not know the rules,
who thought the game was real,
yet I am richer for my loving.

And I will set my mind to knowing
that this will pass;
the wanting,
the unreasoning pain
will grow quiet;
acceptance will come,
will come,
will
come.

II

1990 -2014

The kaleidoscope
is shaken, the images fragment,
something new must grow
from this deep unsettlement -
some other way of being.

Retreat

I

We eat in silence,
the small careful noises
of knife and fork on plate
subdued,
even as our voices
and our outward acts.
But inner silence
is not so easily won.

I think of all the generations
of those who have trodden
the path before me,
striving like me to quiet
the restless wilfulness of mind,
battling with the insidious
petty tyranny of self.
I feel a rueful kinship
with them all.

Then someone begins to read aloud,
concerning the attainments
of the Masters.

II

Necessary things are said,
arrangements made,
civilities to those outside the rule,
but today we are in silence.

Some find that hard to manage,
as if compelled to express
their presence somehow.
Others become less and less obtrusive,
moving with economy, as energy
and even thought are stilled.

As the day goes on
the layers of silence deepen.
In each face is seen
glimpses of the essential self,
the soul's light shining through
the protective mask of every day.
And there comes
a singing in the heart
that needs no words.

Replay

The water in the pool
recycles itself now,
with a sort of
subterranean gurgling sound.

I sit in the place
where you ended your life
and think about that moment;
trying to piece together reasons,
seeking to understand
such dark depths of despair
that only death
could answer it.

The water continues
its intent recycling,
with a momentary beat
before it starts again.

Life flows on through me,
though you who gave me life
are gone.
The pool is different too,
clean and blue,
where once the dead leaves
and the water boatmen floated.

Someone comes to swim,
and the mood shifts,
yet from somewhere unexplored within myself,
there rises up a sort of pain,
catching an echo of the pain you felt,

or the memory of my own,
demanding to be recognised.

◆

The sun is warm on your headstone;
from the schoolyard opposite
the children's voices call.
My face is suddenly wet with tears.
Is it for you who have no need of them,
or for that bewildered schoolgirl
who seems to stand beside me now?
Is it that I must own her as myself -
and have not?

I hear the children's voices
call across the yard,
and feel the slow tears fall.

◆

I go back to the pool
and sit where I sat before,
but today
there are no ghosts.

The water gurgles,
a squirrel poses on the gate-post,
like a heraldic beast;
then I move and he is gone
in a startled, skittering
flash of tail.

Today everything is simply itself
and now.

Patchwork

for my Mother

A winter's evening
and your dear, patient hands -
stiff now with age -
moving among
the coloured scraps of cloth.

The quilt assumes
a living entity around you;
the patchwork of colours,
now sombre,
now jewel-bright,
now blending,
gradually taking
shape and form.
Your life's pattern
spreads out around you,
familiar, yet rich and strange,
uniquely yours.

Textured patterns
in the mellow evening light
and your careful hands
moving among the coloured pieces,
making a whole.

Winter is the Waiting Time

This is the winter of the heart,
knowing the known must end.

You cannot hold it back
                    or shore its ruin up.
So, let it go.

Let it go as gently
                    as last year's leaves –
life withdrawn -
                    drift downward to the earth,
where all seems still and dead.

Yet in the waiting dark within,
the seeds of what's to come
                    begin to stir unseen.

Only assent...
                    and wait.

Pandora's Box

11 September 2001

The twin towers,
symbols of pride and wealth,
crumple before our unbelieving eyes.
Beneath the tomb of masonry
lie fractured lives,
the dead and dying
entangled, twisted
like the jagged edges
of the metal struts.
Everywhere dust falls,
deadening life
with its grey pall.
The air is heavy with it,
raw with pain and shock.

In Jerusalem, the Palestinians
throw sweets to children
early taught to jeer and hate,
who leap and shout,
clenched fists held high,
in triumph at the 'victory'.

While we, just as blind,
daub graffiti on mosque walls,
threaten veiled women quietly
walking their children to school.

When all the evils in
Pandora's box were emptied,
hope alone remained.

So hope we must,
guarding its fragile light
against the remorseless
and encroaching dark.

In the Pitt Rivers Museum [1]

I

In the exhibition space
half-opened packing cases,
a ladder hastily concealed,
pots of paint pushed out of sight.

The staff gathered
self-conscious, uncertain,
providing an audience
for the impromptu ceremony.

First he spoke to the portraits,
welcoming the ancestors,
comforting – explaining
why they had been brought here
to be revered and celebrated.
And then she sang;

a lament that spoke of pain and loss
too deep for tears
and the bearing of it
through long years.

She sang the pain of half a world away
its heart-ache and its beauty,
honouring a past
that will not come again.

II

We who work here
classify, ask about provenance,
tie on neat labels,
conserve, research,
exhibit in carefully considered ways,
instruct, intrigue the eye,
even delight the heart.

Yet when the visitors are gone
and silence falls, the objects
wait to become themselves once more –
their power palpable as breath
in the stillness.

Worlds, far apart in time and space,
meet in arbitrary conjunctions
beneath the glass,
the richness of their stories
locked in silence:
each full of its own life,
breathing hidden histories
into the laden air. Not inimical,
but full of unknown realms
we only glimpse.

In the half-gloom the objects wait
to become themselves once more.

For John

I

I feel your hurt
as if it were my own,
though only your
shuttered look
betrays it.

The longing for the other
simply to be there
aches in the air.

No comfort,
save in the knowledge
of our love, inextricably
the cause of grief
and source of solace.

I am dumb.
Yet my pain
answers yours.

II

Defences gone,
you give yourself
in trusting vulnerability.

I hold the gift
in my two cupped hands
and tremble
lest I do you harm.

III

You are asleep beside me
and I lie, half dreaming,
lazily content –
the summer sunlight
falls across the bed.

Strange that through the body's
urgent dark imperatives
should come such after-stillness.
In that knowing,
beyond shame or reticence,
our true selves meet
and are at one.

Harbinger of Autumn

after Paul Klee

Blocks of cool grey,
mauve and silver
mixed with darker hues,
box and contain
the only splash of colour,
like buildings
shutting out the sun.

Steps and doors,
ways down into
the winding dark
of winter's kingdom.

At the bright centre of it all,
holding the frost at bay,
is what might be
an autumn tree, a leaf, a fruit,
perhaps a pomegranate,
prefiguring Persephone's journey
to the underworld.

Vermeer's Milkmaid

A sturdy figure
intent upon her task
she pours the milk,
caught in an endless present
by the jewelled colours of his brush.

Milk pours from the jug
and if we spoke
she might turn her head to answer,
but her world enfolds her
and our wondering gaze
is silent.

Cezanne's Last Work

Seeing with inward vision,
he sought the hidden affinities.

Rock and tree, water and bathers,
apples, bowl and cloth
flow into each other;

the sharp edge
of separate identity softening
into a harmony of space and line:
a single cosmic whole.

Leaving

I

'Don't' you say, quite firmly,
as I undo the pin clips in your hair
trying to make you comfortable.
One last vanity, those clips
you struggle with each night.
'I don't want to look a fright in the morning'.

You slip into unconsciousness,
hardly breathing.
I see the moment when you leave,
the much-feared ending coming
so gently, taking you unawares
to meet a different morning.

I sit beside you, but as time passes
the body house, untenanted,
has less and less to do with you -
an outworn garment,
old and patched,
and quietly left behind.

II

(5 March 2005)

You'll feel at home here –
at the east end of the Church,
close by the wall,
hearing the children's voices
from the school next door,
absorbed in their own rituals.

The box surprisingly
is heavy: mortal remains
polythene-bagged, incongruous.
I smile despite myself
and seem to catch the echo
of your own ironic look.

Cautioned to take care in the wind,
I kneel to shake the ashes
little by little into the ground.
They fall gently onto rose petals,
rich dark-red rose petals;
we shelter them in a blanket of kind earth.

Snowflakes drift in the chill air,
but we plant snowdrops
and leave daffodils.

III

Loving is never wasted,
though it may seem lost
when those we love are gone.

In that altered landscape
there is only absence,
even the self you were
seems inaccessible.

This valley of the shadow
you must endure.
Only in its darkest heart
will you find its gift.

For your pain is only part
of the world's pain,
your love only part of love itself,
foreshadowing perhaps that vastness
where all love finds its home.

Lazarus

How did it feel
to be drawn back into this life,
commanded to 'come forth'
and leave the world of light?
Did you want to stay,
or was it all too new
and strange?

Martha, Mary,
the Master himself,
all loved you, wept for you.
You must have missed them, too.

Did your body still feel familiar,
the decomposing flesh restored
and owned anew?
In one way, everything
must have seemed the same,
and yet so changed.
How could it not be
after that glimpse
of other realms,
other realities?

It was only four days,
but did you sometimes
secretly long to be there again?

Good Friday Eve

We try to comprehend
that night of desolation.

The church is dark and silent,
stripped of ornament;

the moonlit churchyard,
like the garden at Gethsemane,
shrouded in the mysterious
breathing stillness of night.

Our minds fall away
from the agony and loneliness
of his dark night,
struggling to confirm his will
to what he knew must be,
when all his humanity cried out
that the cup might pass undrunk.

In consent he moves beyond us,
his sacrifice self-chosen and complete:
ancient symbol made present in living flesh.

Seeing clear-eyed all,
all that lay ahead,
Christ let the traitor greet him
with a kiss.

Emptiness

'God's immense blessing can only fit into a heart that is empty'
St John of the Cross

Anatta – the desired goal:
loss of self
in the emptiness
of unknowing.

We fill our hearts
and minds with so much
busyness, so many needs.

Only we can empty them,
can learn to stay
silent in waiting stillness
where the unknown may enter.

Only then can our hearts become
the cup ready to be filled
with grace and blessing.

Just This

be here
be present
just be

hear birdsong
feel the sun on your face
touch the deep flowing wells
of grace eternal

being here
being present
Being

The Last Night

For Elizabeth and Rebecca
In memory of John Whitwick

The night settled around us,
his laboured breathing
the only sound in the dark house.

He cried out once,
the rasping worsening;
she stayed with him until it passed.

Suddenly waking later
from unintended sleep,
she heard only silence.

He'd made no fuss or drama
about his dying,
waiting till we were asleep,
quietly leaving when it was time.

We lit the special anniversary candle
and sat round his dear body
wrapped in the stillness of last sleep.
We prayed and cried,
laughed and remembered,
encircling him with gratitude and love.

Your grace lay on us
as we shared that time:
feeling his presence with us,
yet knowing he was free at last;
the mystery of the moment
holding and enfolding us together.

Christmas Day 2007

Bread and wine,
a bare rock for table,
the sound of gulls and waves
weaving into our prayers,
we share our sacramental feast;
and much-loved, unseen presences
celebrate with us
the new-born Christ.

Here, where sea and sky
blend into one
and the winds blow free,
the separateness of things dissolves
in seamless unity.

Dispossession

I have my suitcase
and a bundle of
clutched possessions.
I have somewhere to go;
here is warmth, shelter, kindness.
Even so, this territory is unfamiliar.
I camp uneasily.

How must it be to be torn
from all that is known?
To see a vanished landscape,
home reduced to rubble
housing the dead.
To flee in terror,
no time to gather precious things,
nothing to anchor you
in your own past.

Survival shuts down other needs.
Huddled families,
children wide-eyed with shock,
crouch miserably together,
seek food,
wait for aid.

How is such displacement borne?
Normality assumes a new face.
The resilient learn to start again,
bravely, patiently, as they can.
But the scars within
cast a long shadow.

'Shakespeare's too difficult...'

Carelessly bestowing beauty
on the second murderer,
conjuring time and place and mood
out of thin air, he spins his magic web
of words; words a good actor
can make us understand intuitively;

words that open windows for us
on life in all its ambiguity:
its foolishness and riches,
its baseness and its wonder;

words that fall on the heart's ear.

But now they say that Shakespeare
is too difficult for schoolchildren,
too hard for them to comprehend.

It's like denying them a key
to life itself.

Jazz

for Iain

The riff anchors it,
then the saxophone takes off;
the improvised phrases
soaring, long and cool,
changing as we listen.

The world you create is ordered,
each thing in its place,
so that those blind hands,
with touch so sensitive
they seem almost to see,
find what they need,
can be in charge.

But here the music takes you
into its own life, the pattern
that is only in the moment –
gone – even as we follow it.

Here, you can be free.

Fish Magic

What did you talk about?
We talked of fish - magic fish –
swimming in occult depths.

We talked of obsession
with the rivers of home,
even in foreign lands,
where other stranger fish
waited to be caught;
of flowing waters
and the moon
moving the tides,
ruling our lives
without our knowing it.

We talked of dreams:
fish that would not die
and the inner agony
of struggling with them;
fish to be feared,
dark, demanding,
powerful.

We talked of goldfish
with their bright beauty,
flickers of red
glimpsed in the muddy depths,
slipping silently, elusively,
between the lotus roots.

Only the patient angler
will catch one.

Life...

Maybe Tracey Emin is right:
life is an unmade bed.
Some of us iron duvet covers,
make neat hospital corners,
create the illusion of control.

But every morning there are
crumpled sheets and pillows –
the whole disorderly
disturbance of living
confronts us all over again.

The Invisible Woman

Imagine her, grieving alone,
reading the formal tributes
to his public life,
knowing all they do not say.

She will not tell their story:
the web of evanescent,
often trivial things
that make a shared life,
even an unseen one.

What was between them
will remain a secret history,
as hidden from the world
as though it had never been.

The Emperor's Tomb

An exhibition at the British Museum

In his tomb they say
all China was replicated:
rivers of mercury, starry constellations,
the land itself.

Here are his courtiers frozen in the moment,
dancers swaying in graceful movement,
musicians playing to bronze swans and ducks,
an archer bending his bow.

His warriors, each individual,
full of life, march
into an eternal present.

Yet their gaze
is on some distant place
beyond the now;

and all that power and beauty
is only the shadowy echo
of his long-vanished world.

Recovery

for J

I

Small white flowers
of Dog's Mercury,
the name at last
etched on my memory,
but when I turn
for your approving smile,
it is not there.

Its absence reopens
the dark well of grief
and I am lost again.

II

'Imagine a place that is
a home for your soul...'
Immediately I am with you,
walking in spring beech woods,
sunlit greenness arching over us.

Here my soul's at home -
in this silent communion,
where I no longer know
which one of us is which.

Revisiting those same woods,
I am shaken with longing
for it to be as it was:
your hand in mine
and we at peace together.

I see the trees
in their green beauty,
hear birdsong,
but no answer.

III

I miss the hard demanding
thereness of you when we were
as close as bodies can be.
I miss the lying peacefully
together afterwards, sharing thoughts
we seemed only to share then.
One of us making tea;
my laughing at the sight of you,
a candlewick-robed emperor
in my dressing gown;
this room our private place,
our kingdom.

I miss waiting to share the trivia of the day.
I miss your going on about
something or other you thought I should do
and the smiling, rueful acceptance
that I wasn't going to,
though that was never said.
I miss catching your eye across the room
and feeling your love
like a visceral shock.
I miss your ability to surprise me,
your acute perception,
your love of beauty;
your insistence on being rational
when reason would not answer;
your anxiety when things weren't right between us
and I couldn't, or wouldn't, say why –
that desperate need not to be shut out.

I miss the things we did together
that were 'our' things:
beech woods in their spring green
amidst drifts of bluebells;
looking at paintings;
champagne and olives for a special treat;
walking hand-in-hand,
you patiently teaching me
to name the wild flowers we saw.

I miss the silently-being-with.

I miss *you*.

IV

Here is my edge:
the place where you are not.

Here will I gently set down
the bundle of our shared days,
or hold you prisoner
in my chains of grief.

Here is the edge.
The cliff falls sheer
into unknown places;
no path is clear.

I will need all my courage
to set out,
to cross this boundary
between past and present
and, with open hand,
welcome the stranger's gift.

V

Grief tears apart,
till you no longer know,
in all its dislocation,
who or what you are.

Recovery is slow,
like convalescence
from long illness;
the set-backs unexpected.

Finally the realization
that you cannot lose
what is truly yours.
All you've become by loving
is deep in your very being.

And you are stronger
than you thought;
life is still good,
kind, funny.
The sun still shines.

VI

The tell-tale props appear:
the crossword, the novel,
refuge of the lonely,
a bastion against pity
or unsought curiosity.

Rejecting such comfort
you become an observer,
spinning stories from the
fleeting glimpses of other lives;
being drawn into those seemingly
random exchanges with strangers,
unlikely to be met again,
when solitude can become -
for a while at least -
intense connection.

VII

Is it enough
to let it be as it is?

Enough just to be here,
where the pain is,
like a wounded animal
making itself still and small,
hoping not to be noticed.

Here you learn patience,
knowing the shadow's fall across the path
will alter with the changing light.

It isn't noble or heroic,
simply all you can do for now.

VIII

Spring beech leaves,
translucent in the sunlight,
droop in gentle vulnerability,

like green butterflies' wings
new released from
their containment.

The alchemy of renewal.

Penelope

An answer to Tennyson's Ulysses

It is decided it seems,
he intends to go;
an old man with adventuring in his veins,
who cannot be at peace.
The kingdom settled,
no more suitors to slay,
Telemachus ready to take over,
what should keep him?

The first time he left I accepted it,
accepted that this was war,
honour was at stake, even though
one really has to wonder if Helen was worth
the years of pain and waste.
Even when the war was ended,
long years of wandering stretched ahead;
twenty years in all that saw
my bloom fade, my hair turn grey.
Who was there then to comfort
the empty nights of bitter weeping,
who to guess how hard-won my calm exterior,
the patient, smiling mistress of a house
over-run with rabble, eager to warm my bed.
He had my heart and I was faithful always.

And now he must set sail again,
testing his ageing body,
seeking out new Scyllas, new Charybdis,
Circe's siren voice still calling him
to challenges unguessed.

The farewell will be public, of course.
It does not even cross his mind
I shall be other than serene and brave;
glad perhaps to set up my loom again
to fill the time till he returns.

But this time there is no way back.
This is where it ends.

Inside the Great Pyramid

Chanting voices drift
down to us as we climb,
strange bird calls
and deep bass notes.
OM resounds around us.

As we crouch to let others pass
on their descent, the lights fail.
In almost total darkness
we grope our way
to the innermost chamber:
that great soaring space,
where Pharaoh's spirit
joined the stars.

The chanting finally stops.
Silence gathers us into itself.
We rest in its stillness,
in the central point,
where the world invisible
touches ours.

To Pallas Athene

Lady of silver-grey olive trees,
your gift to Athens,
hardy, ancient,
bearing rich bounty,
hear our prayer.

Lady of owls,
keen-eyed, silent, deadly;
warrior maiden, sprung fully-armed
from the head of Zeus,
implacable foe to those
who break the law,
we here invoke your aid.

Goddess of Wisdom,
grant us to see
with your grey-eyed clarity;
give us the courage to walk your path,
the way that leads to understanding,
to discernment,
to unflinching truth.

'The Liberated Gods'

from 'Plato's Theology' by Proclus

They move mysteriously,
the boundless ones,
weaving the subtle threads
that hold all things together.

They pass like silent wind
that ripples through the corn,
or clouds dappling the grass with shadows.
Theirs is the silence of the stars at night;
the brightness of the light
beyond the sunlit day,
the rhythm of tides and oceans,
the circling movements of the universe.

The flowing immensity of life
pours through their hands,
shaped into forms and lives,
needs and desires,
cryptic affinities in ether's web
linked in time and space.

Unseen they weave
the hidden threads,
connecting life to all that is.

You

Ineffable, indefinable,
You are also present
in each new-made day,
in the plush purple velvet of this iris,
in the small intent beetle-life
climbing its stalk,
in the stranger's greeting,
in the love of friends.

Unfathomable, mysterious,
vaster than we can conceive,
coming in the tempest,
in the whirlwind of the spirit,
blowing through our smallness,
Yours is the loving presence
that enfolds and holds us.
You are the stillness
which can grace the soul.

We know and do not know,
question and wonder,
worship and fall silent.

You simply are,
within and yet beyond.
The One who is All.

Forgetfulness

We do not understand
we are made of stardust,
fashioned of light
from distant galaxies.
We have forgotten whence we came
and for what reason.

Did we drink too deeply
of the waters of Lethe,
forgetting all that was before?
Or is it being here in bodies
that confuses us?

The way of return
is the way within,
peeling back each onion layer
of our unknowing

till we once more uncover
the inner flame in the soul's deeps,
that light by which we see
the self we do not know,
the self we really are.

Transformations

Confused by reflections
beating its wings against the glass
the butterfly is frantic.

Gently cupping my hands around it,
I will it to know I mean only good.
It quietens and rests -
its imprint so light
it hardly feels as though it's there.

When I open my palms to release it
for a moment or two it stays
opening its peacock wings to the sun,
revealing its softly furred brown body.

Then it's off, flickering
among the flowers,
resting briefly, then gone.

This fragile beauty was once
a voraciously munching caterpillar.
The Haida say butterflies
are the souls of their ancestors;
they dance to do them honour!

Judas

'It feels like a betrayal' you said.
The words lay between us all the day.
The hurt in them was with me
in small, hard knots of misery,
their bitterness more sharp
because so rarely expressed in words.

It is easily accomplished.
Not by intention -
the momentary lapse,
the lack of mindfulness,
and that which cannot be undone
is done.

Justice requires I suffer, too,
though it may be you needed me
for once to know your pain,
even to take the betrayer's part.

Shamanic Journey

The drum beats are insistent: around, below,
above, within me. Honour the sacred space,
honour the earth.

There is the bridge. The drum calls me to cross
into the strange land.

The promised guide is waiting, a wolf, urbane and
suave in a smart jacket. I follow him into the
forest uneasily, thinking of Red Riding Hood.
Soon he deserts me. I am alone in a clearing,
where there is only the beat of the drum.

Comes at last my true guide, an elusive grey
shadow, who calls me to wild places.
We climb steep cliffs and clamber down ravines.
Then, flying high, see far, far into the distance. We
rest by a still lake where other wolf kind can be
glimpsed along the shore. Then on again, freer,
faster, deeper into his world.

The drum note changes; summons me back across
the bridge. I must return.

He smiles farewell, my wolf brother; is gone.

Dancing at Hawkwood

'So let us dance', he said,
and dance we did.
Hesitantly at first,
then moving, flowing with the music,
each of us flowering into our own dance:
some self-contained,
some reaching out to others,
some partners briefly
as the moment took them.

From deep within came a desire
somehow to be blessing,
to let it flow through us to each other
and out beyond the confines of the room,
to the smiling sunlit earth
and all its creatures;
that we might be fully part
of the dance that was dancing us,
the dance of life itself.

Homelessness

for Bev

They are homeless, unlovely,
wandering on the verges,
separated from themselves and us.
And you among them
welcoming their shadows,
finding in their darkness
a place for your own voice.

Within you is a howl
that will be heard.
A howl of the world's pain:
of separation and of need,
and the terror of being lost,
alone in the engulfing dark.

The way back is reconnection -
with the earth and those around you.
A way of gentleness and kindliness
to heal the wounded self
and make it whole.

The Rampant Feminist

Men can be such prats.
They behave abominably,
then carry on as though nothing had happened.
No word of explanation or apology.

We, on the other hand,
are expected to understand,
forgive, forbear... Maybe,
when I was young.

Now I think being aware
of someone else's feelings
is simple good manners;
ignoring them is not an option.

Timeslip

Memory has not played false.

The sweeping movement of downland
crouches like an animal at rest,
a patchwork of fields and farms below.

Bright poppies in the grain beside the path,
skylarks spiralling overhead
fill the air with song.

The sun is warm on my back.
Time scarcely disturbs the grass.

Wittenham Clumps, Oxfordshire

Climbing this ancient hill
the wind catches my breath,
the landscape opens out below,
winter-coloured fields charged
with that indefinable sense
of coming change:
the earth seems more alive,
the sky a brighter blue.

Above me the ring of trees,
the place of power.
Out of nowhere a kite swoops,
a flying dragon, full of *chi*,
tail streaming as the wind takes it,
circling, spiralling, never still,
riding the air triumphant;
life energy,
raw, inexhaustible.

Carpe Diem

Nature can be so winter elegant.
The thin outline of leafless trees,
against a palest shell pink
skeined with grey cloud.
The deep mysterious green
of sky on frosty nights, after the sun has set;
hoar frost silvering the twigs and boughs
with intricate patterns,
grasses rigid with the cold.
Look, oh look, before it vanishes.

Overnight the snow comes.
We watch children build igloos and snowmen,
dodge snow balls surprising in their hardness,
relive the wild joy of tobogganing downhill
gathering speed, oblivious of cold and wet,
knowing only the magical kingdom of *now*.

Easter Sunday: Magdalene Remembers

You ask how it was that day...
You have to remember how it had been.
We'd seen the Master die,
shared the hurried burial rites
and the long, long hours of an endless Shabbat
when we could do nothing.
We had no idea what might happen. We were terrified,
bruised, stunned with the speed and horror of it all.
Everything was at an end.

It was still dark when I set out that morning –
I couldn't bear to wait any longer. And then
to discover they couldn't leave him alone even in death –
the stone had been pushed aside, the tomb was empty.
I ran so fast to tell the others that there was no breath
to keep up on the way back – they far outran me -
while I stumbled, blinded with tears and frantic
because they had taken my Lord away.

At last I realized that I was alone in the garden.
I made myself look deep into the tomb,
as if some vestige of him might still be there.
Two figures, full of light, sitting like guardians,
asked why I was weeping. Then a voice behind me
asked the same thing and who was I looking for?
I thought it was the gardener and begged him
to tell me where the body was.

And then he said my name, just my name,
'Mary', he said, and I knew,
I knew beyond doubt it was the Master

standing there, half-smiling at me,
with that look I loved so much,
which seemed to see and understand everything.

I cried out in joy and wonder,
reaching out my hands to him,
but he would not let me touch him.
He said: 'I have not yet ascended'.
But he gave me a message for the others
that now he must return home, to his Father and ours.
Then he was gone.

It was almost like a dream,
but I knew it had happened. I knew
because of the way he said my name.
When I found the others, all I could do was babble:
'I have seen the Lord, I have seen him!'

Being Real

for J

With you there was no need
to pretend, or be other than I am,
indeed I could not be -
what we shared had to ring true.
Ironic though it might seem,
honesty was our touchstone;
in it lay our integrity.

The struggle to find that core of who we are
is what makes us fully human.
It is the journey we each must make
into the labyrinth of unknown self,
venturing alone
into its twists and turnings,
knowing the minotaur is there,
waiting for us
in the listening dark.

But when at last we face him,
it is only to discover
he is our own shadow,
blocking out the sun.

'The Self deep-seated in the heart' [2]

The question was:
'How do you think of God?'
I struggled to answer.

Later, from deep within
beyond the words, these well up:

God is the unfolding path
as well as the end
of a never-ending journey;
the straightest route
and all the wandering byways
of the human heart.

There is nowhere He is not,
nothing we can do
that He's not part of,
nothing, no one, His loving providence
does not embrace and hold,
just as it is,
and in its infinite potentiality,
just as we are,
and as we will be.

Christmas Eve

It's a myth, of course –
the star, the three wise men,
the angels, the shepherds,
the baby laid in a manger
because there was no room at the inn,
the Virgin birth, the animals talking,
even Father Christmas.
Stories told round the fire
to warm the winter's cold
and keep the dark at bay.

But what if it were true?
God helpless as a tiny baby,
that mean stable holding the crown of all the earth.

What if they did come,
summoned by angels, led by a star,
to bring their gifts and worship?
What if the second coming is now,
means Christ born in the heart,
born here, now, in each of us?

Surely this night of all nights
the stars seem brighter
and joyous angel voices
fill the waiting stillness of the skies.

Stop and listen to their song.

Griffin's Point, Cornwall

Here, round this headland
where the wind bends the stunted gorse
and threads birdsong through
thrift and close-cropped turf,
the sea is never still.

Past and future slide into
its ceaseless rhythm,
till there is only an endless now -
a state of being, of knowing,
that all is as it should be.

Life is simply as it is,
stranger than we think,
more dangerous,
more beautiful.

Otters [3]

Lithe and intent
the 'shadow of the stream'
slips into the water,
swimming so sleekly
there's hardly a ripple.

Eyes beady bright
missing nothing,
almost smiling;
two water creatures
diving, intertwining,
surprising each other
in a joyous game,
boneless and enchanting.

Giveaway

'I need to give away my life'.
Asked what you mean,
you simply shake your head.
The words linger in the air,
waiting to be understood.

Is it an offering to life
of all you've gained;
a need to say 'this is who I am,
who I have become',
then let even that fall away?

In one sense maybe nothing matters
as much as we thought it did,
yet each never-to-be-repeated moment
is infinitely precious;

through it the timeless
pours the gift of time,
endlessly renewed
even as it vanishes.

Now

The immediately necessary
is so dominant:
we let it crowd out
what we most want to do,
allowing its urgent trivialities
to devour the minutes.

The paradox is ,
now there is less time,
it seems more important
simply to be here;

to look at this world,
with a child's absorbed delight,
as though its wonder
was all that mattered.

Miracles

Spendthrift you might call it,
as if this autumn blaze of colour
were an accidental afterthought,
but the tree knows deep within
when the sun's warmth wanes,
knows it is time to rest.

The cells, through which all summer
life has flowed, become impermeable;
each leaf, its work now done,
separates from the tree, ready to fall,
to become leaf mould.

Yet hidden under green chlorophyll,
lie other pigments,
carotene, xanthophyll, anthocyanin,
waiting to blossom into coloured glory -
orange and gold and bronze and fiery red -
a dying splendour flung before our eyes,
burnished by sunlight,
softened, almost luminous,
in mist and rain.

Wind-blown leaves dance awhile,
then lie in a rich carpet at our feet.

Wordplay

Sometimes there are no words
to say what you really want to say:
ideas refuse to be expressed,
phrases tease, elude;
the passing moment slides away,
its nuances, its thereness, gone
before you can begin to capture it.

Then you can only wait.
Wait until the words
decide to play once more.

Venice

You need an artist's eye to capture
the play of light on the water,
the ripples of a passing boat,
the harmony of proportion.

Whistler got it, and Turner:
the subtle shifts and changes,
mist and shadow,
reflections shimmering
with the tide's sway.

Palazzos gently sinking
under the weight of their own history,
dwarfed by passing liners,
the decay, the cranes, the tourists,
all are part of it.

The city deceives,
confusing you with twists and turns
until arriving no longer seems to matter.
Round the corner, over the bridge,
in the glimpsed courtyard,
the unexpected waits
to weave its spell of colour
and grace and light.
The senses dazzle.

Giverny

I like to think of Monet in his garden,
obsessed with light and colour,
creating a living work of art.

The garden gently absorbs us,
slowing the hoards of visitors,
until they stop and let it speak.

Rain and summer sun conspire
in a profusion of such richness –
irises, peonies, roses -
their colours burn into the mind.
Drunk with the feast,
for a moment we see as he did.

Here he laboured and painted,
painted and repainted
until the life force within
blossomed on the canvas –
inner and outer seeing
fused into one.

Mindfulness

There are days when you come to sit
reluctantly, inwardly fidgeting,
the monkey mind distracted,
skittering about.
All you can do is sit
noticing what happens,
returning your attention
again and again
to the anchor of the breath.

Yet sometimes the moment
simply enfolds you;
thoughts pass like drifting clouds,
unable to disturb the place
where silence winds you
deep into itself.

It doesn't seem to matter
whether you struggle or not,
so long as you allow
whatever is
to be as it is
and sit with it.

That is the unexpected grace.

Walkabout

Australian Aboriginal Art at the RA

Ancestral beings shaped the land –
are the land;
cross-hatched in glowing power
their life energy shimmers through it.

In the birthing place
the sand dunes shift and dance
in rippling ridges,
like a serpent's trail -
a rainbow serpent
birthing the world.

We saw landscape, challenge;
haunting, unsettling beauty,
the desolation of the outback
that must be tamed. Unread
the coded messages:
possum tracks, a wallaby,
sacred water holes,
the dance of rain,
where home is everywhere
and nowhere.

Père Lachaise Cemetery [4]

We never did find Héloïse and Abélard
as we wandered among quiet tomb-houses,
where famous and unknown alike
share the equality of death.

Some deep instinct draws us to be near
those with whom we feel connection,
who live in our remembrance,
our enrichment.

In a peaceful, sunlit corner,
full of birdsong and spring green,
towers the dark monument to Dachau,
chilling the warm day.

There is no recompense
to heal such loss
till each of us has faced
the darkness in the heart.

I remember a small white feather,
captured in its fall in Hagia Sophia,
and the young man who smiled and said:
'I think it is for peace. Keep it.'

An angel passing, or a feather of Maat's,
to weight the final balance?

Prayer

May the wind of the Spirit
blow through my smallness.

May the vast unknowable
wonder of life challenge
all my careful containments.

May the journey within
and the journey without
become a single path;

a returning to the centre,
to the heart,
a coming home.

NOTES

1. In the Pitt Rivers Museum

The Pitt Rivers Museum is Oxford University's Museum of Anthropology and Archaeology. The first poem was written after a visit from Sir Hugh and Lady Kawfaru. Sir Hugh was a patron and a lawyer and both of them tirelessly worked for their people's rights and culture. He performed a Maori greeting ceremony before the opening of a photographic exhibition.

The second poem was inspired partly by the very special atmosphere the museum has when the visitors leave and partly by the response of a Haida visitor to the objects of other cultures. She was deeply concerned that she did not know how to respond to them correctly.

2. 'The Self deep-seated in the heart'

Words of Sri Krishna, from A Synthesis of the Bhagavad-Gita, published by The Shrine of Wisdom, available from The Fintry Trust.

3. Otters

I caught a snippet of a programme about Northumberland that called otters 'the shadow of the stream'.

4. Père Lachaise

A corner of the cemetery is dedicated to those who were deported to concentration camps in the 1940s. Each camp has its own monument where all that could be interred was some dust and ashes. On one were the words that the dead would never be avenged until 'tu ne tueras pas'. There is no way in English to capture the immediacy of that 'tu'.

Hagia Sophia is the Church of the Holy Wisdom, which was later converted into a Mosque, until Mustafa Kemal Ataturk decreed it should be neither and both and turned it into a museum. Sadly this unity is now threatened.

In Egyptian mythology the soul after departing this life was weighed against the Feather of Truth, the feather of the goddess Maat.

LIST OF TITLES